IDAHO *wild and beautiful*

Featuring the photography of Steve Bly and Leland Howard

Farcountry Press

Right: Old-growth forest in the panhandle's Kaniksu National Forest. LELAND HOWARD

Title page: Baron Peak in central Idaho's Sawtooth Mountains. STEVE BLY

Front cover: Imogene Lake in the Sawtooth Wilderness Area. LELAND HOWARD

Back cover: The Idaho Capitol glows on Boise's skyline during a soft summer night. STEVE BLY

ISBN 1-56037-164-1

Photography © 2000 Steve Bly, Leland Howard and Tim Christie
© 2000 Farcountry Press

For more information on our books write: Farcountry Press, P.O. Box 5630, Helena, MT 59604, call: (800) 654-1105, or visit www.montanamagazine.com

Printed in Hong Kong

Steve Bly

I never picked up a camera until I was forty-five. Creativity and art had never occurred to me. But Idaho had, in a big way.

Three high school buddies and I drove out from Kansas in a '49 Chevy, some time ago. That was an eye-opener, let me tell you. After working on summer jobs in the Northwest I vowed to return.

I became Director of Idaho State Parks and then Assistant Director of Washington State Parks. Not until I became Director of Tourism for The Boise Convention & Visitors Bureau did I look a camera in the eye. There was no one else to take promotional pictures. The weird gizmo with its slick tongue of film jumped into my hands. That became my best and most enduring professional challenge.

Early one October morning I took my camera to the Bruneau sand dunes. I was alone in the mist, surrounded by the tints and hues of the awakening day, and it was an intense experience. Geese flew overhead; waterfowl skimmed the lakes. That was the day I decided to become a full-time photographer. My horoscope matched my soaring spirits, and I made the jump to bodies, lenses, tripods, filters— bam! bam! bam!—exclusively, and I have been shooting like a madman ever since.

In Idaho, if you like the outdoors, that's not a difficult thing to do. Less than a million and a half people inhabit its dusty and green, plunging and climbing 83,557 miles that make it the thirteenth-largest state. About seventy percent is protected federal and state land. The geographic diversity is immense. We have the Craters of the Moon ("The strangest seventy-five square miles on the North American continent"); the City of Rocks, where climbers from all over the world ascend Bread Loaves, Elephant Rock and Twin Sisters; brawny, sudsy, lion-colored Hells Canyon, the deepest canyon in North America; by far the most whitewater river miles of any state; outstanding ski resorts and outback snow territory; vast deserts; mountain ranges that scratch the sky; and large, beautiful lakes.

I'm not a landscape purist, and try to include people as much as possible in my pictures. I want to see their faces and enjoyment for the territory.

Since that first "hot potato" of a camera unexpectedly leapt into my hands, largely through teaching myself and a whole lot of experience, my photography has improved. Photo assignments for books and magazines have taken me around the globe. But getting back to Idaho is always special to me. Photography changed my life, how I see things, the light, color and composition of my surroundings. The way I understand people; the web of life. And I couldn't be in a better place than Idaho to act upon these discoveries.

The Boise River is a flyfisher's paradise. STEVE BLY

The South Fork of the Snake River flows through Idaho Falls, whose Mormon temple spire rises on the horizon. LELAND HOWARD

Leland Howard

If you photograph what you care about, it will show in your images.

One of the most difficult ways to make a living as a photographer is to shoot wilderness images. Not only is the competition intense and the market limited, but such hardships as climbing a mountain in the pre-dawn darkness and adjusting camera settings with freezing, shaking hands are commonplace. To do it well, to do it without tiring of the fresh insights that wild places offer, requires a special mind-set and a heart that never ceases to be moved by what the eyes see.

Idaho is a phenomenal place. I am fortunate to call this varied and often astonishing region my home. After years of exploring and photographing its wonders, I am still surprised by its sudden changes in mood and terrain. Idaho is difficult to describe without making it seem unreal. Violent volcanoes, passing ice ages, and massive floods have shaped the land, setting the stage for an exceptionally diverse environment.

Deserts and snowcapped peaks live side by side, bearing names given them by intrepid early explorers: Lost River Valley, Craters of the Moon, Snake River, Tin Cup Mountain. These are the features of an unparalleled inland empire, as colorful and eccentric as the names imply. My challenge is to do them justice.

I think of photographing Idaho's lands as the art of painting with light.

I am not alone in my appreciation of the land. It seems that everyone who lives here has a story about a place they visit for solitude and peace. Most of the time they are happy to direct me to a favorite spot, though following the directions can be hard. "Just as you cross over that ridge, keep a lookout on your right, there's a dim road there. Take it till it ends, then keep goin'. You'll cross a dry lake bed, then it gets rough. Go about another mile or two, then you should be able to see the edge of the canyon. It's a tough walk down in, but there's nothin' like it!"

Idaho was the last of the fifty states to be entered by white men, and it is still a very rough and tumble territory in many ways. Some areas can be accessed only by hiking, backpacking and cross-country skiing. I have carried camera gear to places where mountain goats fear to tread. With more than five million acres of designated wilderness, more than three thousand whitewater river miles, and eighty mountain ranges, I still have a lot of territory to cover, though I've been working on it for more than twenty years.

As the sole photographer for two Continental Divide Trail books, I recently added 1,300 more miles to my tally of wild country that I've explored on foot. And I'll keep on going.

Right: The east fork of the Owyhee River cuts a deep southwest Idaho canyon. LELAND HOWARD

Below: Winter magic on cottonwood trees. LELAND HOWARD

Above: Late autumn snow dusts the Frank Church Wilderness Area. LELAND HOWARD

Right: In central Idaho's Pioneer Mountains, arrowleaf balsamroot's bright yellow contrasts with lupine. LELAND HOWARD

Above: *A peaceful paddle on Lake Coeur d'Alene.* STEVE BLY

Facing page: Providing a hiker's welcome on summer days is Fern Falls, Coeur d'Alene National Forest. LELAND HOWARD

Sundown's spectacular moment on the Sawtooth Mountains above Trail Creek Lake. STEVE BLY

Below: On the Stonebraker Ranch in Chamberlain Basin. STEVE BLY

Facing page: Traditional Basque dress and a sheepherder's wagon recall the immigrants once attracted by Idaho's sheep industry. STEVE BLY

Left: A corporation sponsors Fourth of July fireworks in Idaho Falls. LELAND HOWARD

Below: Situated in Boise, the Idaho State Capitol took from 1905 to 1920 to build. STEVE BLY

Right: Located on the south end of Payette Lake, McCall is a water-recreation mecca. STEVE BLY

Below: Bald eagle demonstrating his majesty on a Sawtooth National Recreation Area perch. STEVE BLY

Above: Jewels in the mist at Upper Mesa Falls on Henry's Fork of the Snake River. STEVE BLY

Right: Sunset's eerie glow over the Sawtooth National Recreation Area, central Idaho. LELAND HOWARD

Above: Cache National Forest in southeast Idaho. LELAND HOWARD

Right: Having survived the Oregon Trail as far as Register Rock, pioneers used axle grease to proclaim their progress. Today, City of Rocks National Reserve (facing page) protects the site. LELAND HOWARD

Right: Wild Idaho is home to cougars. STEVE BLY

Below: On the Blackfoot River in southeast Idaho. LELAND HOWARD

Facing page: Coulter's lupine in the Lemhi Mountains, which once were the Shoshone Indians' haven from enemies. LELAND HOWARD

Above: A golden eagle in for the landing at Snake River Birds of Prey Area. STEVE BLY

Right: A brilliant display of sky rocket. LELAND HOWARD

Facing page: Mind-boggling granite shapes in City of Rocks National Reserve.
LELAND HOWARD

Right: Taking advantage of a sunny autumn day at Beavers Ponds, Sun Valley. STEVE BLY

Below: Cold but still flowing: the Buffalo River at Island Park. LELAND HOWARD

Above: Chipmunk's snack-time in Ponderosa State Park.

STEVE BLY

Left: A Beaverhead Range bouquet of wildflowers.

LELAND HOWARD

Facing page: High mountain lake in the Lemhi Mountains.

LELAND HOWARD

Above: The "Niagara of the West,"
Shoshone Falls of the Snake River
at Twin Falls. STEVE BLY

Right: Endless fenceline near McCall.
STEVE BLY

Facing page: Fair weather tomorrow, or so
sunset proclaims over Lake Pend Oreille.
LELAND HOWARD

Preceding pages: Camas Prairie Wildlife Marsh of central Idaho once provided Indians with the camas bulb, a dietary staple. STEVE BLY

Below: Near Cataldo, Old Mission State Park holds the Mission of the Sacred Heart, built by Coeur d'Alene Indians and Catholic missionaries from 1848 to 1853. STEVE BLY

Facing page: Paintbrush accents grow below a southwest Idaho rock tower that marked an Oregon Trail cutoff. LELAND HOWARD

Right: Sawtooth Mountains beauty. STEVE BLY

Below: Skiing season is drawing near at Sun Valley. STEVE BLY

Above: Uh, I don't know, Dad—maybe I'll just play basketball. STEVE BLY

Facing page: The Cub River charges through southeast Idaho. LELAND HOWARD

Above: Targhee National Forest in winter spangles.
LELAND HOWARD

Right: Neck and tail feathers spread dramatically make this ruffed grouse a hen's dreamboy. TIM CHRISTIE

Facing page: A quiet Boise River's autumn path through the capital city. STEVE BLY

Below: Snake River Valley storm. LELAND HOWARD

Right: Beargrass blossoms greet the morning, Coeur d'Alene National Forest. LELAND HOWARD

Above: Bergdorf Hot Springs, near McCall. STEVE BLY

Left: Pass Lake, high in central Idaho's Lost River Range. LELAND HOWARD

Right: Storm clouds move over the Montana border above the Beaverhead Mountains of the Bitterroot Range. LELAND HOWARD

Below: Selway River excitement. STEVE BLY

Above: Just hanging on, in the Twin Falls area. STEVE BLY

Right: Bruneau Dunes State Park. STEVE BLY

74

Above: Lemhi Valley charcoal kilns. LELAND HOWARD

Left: Arrowleaf balsamroot backed by paintbrush and lupine.
LELAND HOWARD

Facing page: Cold silence on the Buffalo River. LELAND HOWARD

Right: Trying out brand-new wings above Canyon County farmland. STEVE BLY

Below: Summer symphony at Kimmel Creek. STEVE BLY

Above: At the Shoshone-Bannock powwow, now in its fourth decade. STEVE BLY

Right: A bull elk bugles to attract some sweethearts. STEVE BLY

Facing page: Clearwater National Forest silhouettes. LELAND HOWARD

Below: Southwest Idaho's rugged Bruneau Canyon. STEVE BLY

Facing page: Day's end at Craters of the Moon National Monument. LELAND HOWARD

Following pages: Fire danger from above, at an eastern Idaho wheatfield. STEVE BLY

Near right: A surviving "little house out back," in Little Lost Valley. LELAND HOWARD

Far right: Hells Canyon of the Snake River includes North America's deepest gorge. STEVE BLY

Below: Looking across the state border to Wyoming's Teton Range. LELAND HOWARD

Right: In the White Cloud Mountains of central Idaho. LELAND HOWARD

Below: A misty morning in Harriman State Park. STEVE BLY

Left: Cracking the whip for real in the Carey-Kimama Desert. STEVE BLY

Below: Skyline of Boise, capital and business center of Idaho. STEVE BLY

Right: A Salmon River homestead near Riggin. STEVE BLY

Below: Autumn palette in Grand Targhee National Forest. STEVE BLY

Following pages: Casting in Fall Creek Falls at the Snake River. STEVE BLY

Above: Idaho's highest mountain, 12,662-foot Borah Peak, was named for prominent U.S. Senator William Borah (1865-1940). LELAND HOWARD

Right: Watchful male mallard duck. STEVE BLY

Facing page: The panhandle's St. Joe River.
LELAND HOWARD

Right: Night skiing at Bogus Basin Ski Area, with Boise in the distance. STEVE BLY

Below: Mirror Lake in Hells Canyon Wilderness Area lives up to its name. LELAND HOWARD

Above: Early touches of autumn in east Idaho's Palisades area. LELAND HOWARD

Facing page: Caribou Mountains grain a-ripening. LELAND HOWARD

Left: Packing in past Baron Lake in the Sawtooth National Recreation Area. STEVE BLY

Below: Cut-bow trout like this one are hybrids of cutthroats and rainbows. STEVE BLY

Above: Climber's meditation, City of Rocks National Reserve. LELAND HOWARD

Facing page: Upper Priest Falls forms a wood-eating eddy, Kaniksu National Forest. LELAND HOWARD

Right: The Upper Priest River runs through a northern Idaho rainstorm. LELAND HOWARD

Below: Poppies in Sun Valley. STEVE BLY

Facing page: In and above an autumn storm raking the Snake River Mountains. LELAND HOWARD

Below: In central Idaho, an abandoned homestead. STEVE BLY

Left: Looking down onto the South Fork, Snake River. STEVE BLY

Below: Lively autumn welcome to Targhee National Forest. STEVE BLY

Above: Camas Prairie spring mosaic. STEVE BLY

Right: Idaho homestead just west of the Tetons. LELAND HOWARD